GOOD DRINKS

DRINKS

for

BAD

DAYS

Kerry Colburn

HOLIDAY EDITION

SASQUATCH
BOOKS

Printed in Canada
Published by Sasquatch Books
Distributed by PGW/Perseus
15 14 13 12 11 10 09   10 9 8 7 6 5 4 3 2 1

Cover illustrations: Sarah Plein
Cover design: Henry Quiroga
Interior design: Henry Quiroga
Interior illustrations: Kate Quinby

Library of Congress Cataloging-in-Publication Data
Colburn, Kerry.
  Good drinks for bad days. Holiday edition / Kerry Colburn.
      p. cm.
  ISBN-13: 978-1-57061-621-1
  ISBN-10: 1-57061-621-3
1. Cocktails. 2. Cocktails--Humor. 3. Holiday cookery. I. Title. II. Title: Holiday edition.
  TX951.C7226 2009
  641.8'74--dc22

                              2009017769

Sasquatch Books
119 South Main Street, Suite 400
Seattle, WA 98104
(206) 467-4300
www.sasquatchbooks.com
custserv@sasquatchbooks.com

TABLE *of* CONTENTS

Remedies for the Rest of the Year ... 79

Index ... 102

Introduction

Ho ho . . . oh, no!

It's a universal truth that the holiday season comes festively packaged with a vast assortment of disasters, both big and small. And despite your best intentions, you will fall victim to many of them. How could you possibly escape? This time of year is nuttier than a fruitcake: family fights, extra pounds, money woes, end-of-year deadlines, stressful shopping, horrible traffic, and no date for the holiday party. It's enough to make even the most positive holiday elf a little — well, Grinch-like. Whatever your life is like the rest of the year, chances are you'll experience more than your share of bad days between Thanksgiving and New Year's. What to do? Drink, of course!

Luckily, the holidays are also rife with excuses and opportunities to merrily knock back a few extra cocktails. So make them count. On these pages you'll find a wide variety of antidotes to all your holiday frustrations. Did your boss shaft you at holiday bonus time? Was your luggage lost and your flight delayed? Did your significant other give you the worst gift imaginable? Is your entire family staying with you? Singing Christmas carols and baking cookies ain't gonna help, my friend. This is no time to get in the spirit. It's time to break out the hard stuff.

So turn off the phone, ignore that stack of unaddressed holiday cards, and put on your fat pants. Toast to the fact that the year is coming to a close, and the next one will most certainly be better. After a few sips, you might actually believe it! (After all, it is the season to believe.)

Cheers!

Glassware & Garnishes

Let's get one thing straight: there are days so heinous that what you drink (and how quickly you can fix it) is infinitely more important than what you drink it out of. On those occasions, some booze dumped into store-bought eggnog and drunk straight out of the carton might not be out of the question. But, when possible, the proper glass and garnish can elevate your cocktail—and your mood. So, if you've got access to the proper tools in your house, treat yourself to a nicely executed beverage now and then—you deserve it, especially this time of year. Here are some bar basics to help you along:

Glassware

Champagne flute [⚲]: Designed with a tall, narrow opening to retain effervescence, this is the glass of choice for any bubbly cocktail.

Cocktail glass [⚥]: Also called a martini glass, this sophisticated stemmed glass is the one to use for shaken or stirred cocktails.

Highball glass [▯]: Also called a Collins glass, this tall, straight-sided glass is the most versatile for your bar, perfect for any long drink (and for making short drinks into long drinks).

Old-fashioned glass [▯]: Another handy glass to have on hand, this one is short and stout with a heavy bottom, ideal for any drink on the rocks. (Also called a rocks glass, tumbler, or whiskey glass; the larger version is a double old-fashioned.)

Shot glass [▽]: For cutting to the chase, there's no substitute for a shot, no chaser. This two-ounce bad boy is your go-to glass when even ice seems extraneous.

Wine glass [⚲]: A wine glass, especially a larger goblet-style one, is a nice choice for punch or any tropical or frozen drink. It can also be used as a change of scene for a highball.

Beer mug [⬛]: 'Nuff said. (To take it up a notch, put it in the freezer before using.)

Pint glass [⬛]: This tapered, pint-size glass with no handle is usually reserved for beer or hard cider (it's best not to use a pint glass for a mixed drink unless you really mean business).

Brandy snifter [♀]: This short-stemmed glass with its very round bowl is ideal for swirling and sniffing the good stuff—brandy, liqueurs, and Cognacs—and for feeling superior.

Garnishes

Most garnishes are straightforward: just slice a wedge of lime or grab a few raspberries and toss them in your drink. But here's a quick primer for when you're going a bit more highbrow.

Twist: If a drink calls for a twist, use a paring knife to cut an approximately 2-inch strip of peel from a washed piece of citrus, avoiding as much of the pith as possible. Twist the peel just above the drink, then run it around the rim (if desired) and drop it in.

Spiral: A longer version of the twist, this streamer-like curlicue adds festive panache to a cocktail. Use a vegetable peeler or paring knife to remove a thin, continuous peel from one end of the fruit to the other, then twist it around your finger and drop it in the drink.

Slices and wheels: When a drink calls for a fruit slice or wheel, use a sharp paring knife to cut off the end of the fruit and then cut a crosswise segment about ¼ inch wide. To use as a garnish, cut a slice in the wheel and balance on the side of the glass.

Salted or sugared rims: To salt or sugar a rim, coat the rim of the glass with a citrus wedge and then dunk it onto a small plate or bowl of salt or superfine sugar. Turn gently to distribute, shake off any excess, and then carefully pour in your cocktail.

GOOD DRINKS FOR BAD DAYS:

HOLIDAY EDITION

Bad Day: *Family fight*

What with all that holiday cheer, it's now uncertain how the argument even started. Was it the unfavorable comment about Aunt Peggy's new boyfriend? Uncle Chip's third martini? Cousin Andy's lack of a job? The undercooked turkey? The forgotten whipped cream? Oh, who can remember? But before you knew it, the gloves were off: leave it to your family to really let 'er rip. The bad news is that everyone left in a huff. The good news is you now have the house (and the leftovers) to yourself. Time to tap out with something that packs a punch even more powerful than your mother-in-law's.

Good Drink: *Planter's Punch*

2 ounces dark rum
Dash of Cointreau
1½ ounces fresh orange juice
1½ ounces fresh pineapple juice
½ ounce fresh lime juice
½ ounce simple syrup*
Dash of grenadine
Orange slice and maraschino cherry for garnish

Shake rum, Cointreau, orange juice, pineapple juice, lime juice, simple syrup, and grenadine with ice, then strain into an ice-filled highball glass. Garnish with orange slice and cherry. Drink while thinking of clever barbs you *should've* said.

*Make the simple syrup by stirring 2 parts granulated sugar into 1 part hot water and letting the sugar dissolve completely. Cool before using.

From Bad to Worse: **No one had the decency to leave? Multiply the recipe by the number of angry people and serve in a large pitcher.**

Bad Day: *Gave totally wrong gift*

Your significant other gave you an expensive watch with a lovely sentiment engraved on the back. You, on the other hand, offered your sweetie a $20 Gap gift card, flowers from the grocery store, or an ill-fitting item from a sale rack. Ouch. You will likely never forget the look of utter disappointment that accompanied the opening of your poorly wrapped box. At least you'll have another chance to impress on Valentine's Day . . . of course, you might be single by then. Might as well start drowning your sorrows now; you're in for a lonely night.

Good Drink: *Lonely Night*

¾ ounce coffee liqueur
1¼ ounce Baileys or other Irish cream liqueur
1¼ ounce hazelnut liqueur
1 scoop vanilla ice cream
Whipped cream

Combine the coffee liqueur, Baileys, hazelnut liqueur, and ice cream in a blender with one scoop of ice and blend until smooth. Pour into a cocktail glass. Top with whipped cream.

From Bad to Worse: If you actually re-gifted—and were found out—make yourself two drinks and polish off the rest of the ice cream. You'll be lonely for a while.

Bad Day: *Snowed in*

When you're not sure whether that's your car or an enormous white elephant in the driveway, you know the weather is going to pose a challenge. Of course, this is probably the day that you absolutely must get to a holiday event, the airport, or a crucial appointment across town. This isn't the time to try to clean your windshield with a credit card, this is serious. You need to find two gloves with no holes in them, boots, a shovel, a proper ice scraper . . . oh, it's just too much. Make some cinnamon toast, cancel everything, and celebrate the winter wonderland with a snowstorm of a different sort—an *indoor* one.

Good Drink: *Blizzard*

1 ounce brandy
1 ounce Baileys or other Irish cream liqueur
1 ounce coffee liqueur
1 ounce white rum
2 scoops vanilla ice cream
1 splash light cream
Dash of nutmeg

Pour the brandy, Baileys, coffee liqueur, rum, ice cream, and cream into a blender. Blend until smooth. Pour into a large brandy snifter, dust with nutmeg, and serve while watching the snow come down.

Bad Day: *Haven't mailed holiday cards*

There they sit, on your coffee table, where they've lived for the past three weeks. Taunting you. In a fit of industriousness, you bought six boxes of holiday cards, along with some festive stamps and return address labels. So what's stopping you? Somehow, night after night, you opt to do almost anything in order to put off this task. You've even cleaned your kitchen and called your mother. If you need a fresh way to procrastinate tonight, try liquor. Fire up a modern cocktail with an old-fashioned name, and toast alternative forms of communication.

Good Drink: *Cablegram*

2 ounces blended whiskey
1 teaspoon powdered sugar
Juice of ½ lemon
3 to 5 ounces ginger ale

Stir whiskey, powdered sugar, and lemon juice with ice in a highball glass. Add ginger ale to taste and stir gently.

Bad Day: *Holiday traffic*

Somehow, everywhere you go this holiday season, you're
stuck in a long line of cars. What is with all this congestion on
the freeway? Where is everybody going? And why is it always
worst when you're running late? Whether you're trying to
get to a party before the booze runs out or the mall before
it closes, there is nothing worse than the seemingly endless
stop-and-go that is holiday traffic. When you finally do get
out of the car, it's time to reward yourself with a different
kind of sloe driver.

Good Drink: *Sloe Driver*

1½ ounces sloe gin
5 ounces orange juice

Pour gin and orange juice over ice into a highball glass. Drink while making offensive gestures at imaginary cars.

Bad Day: *Stuck at home while friends travel*

It's enough to make anyone blue. Several of your friends
are off on a lovely tropical vacation—Hawaii, Mexico, the
Caribbean, what's the difference?—and you're happy for
them. Sure you are! But meanwhile, where does that leave
you? Stuck in your usual routine: apartment, traffic, cubicle,
meetings, TV. And it's cold! When the beach, palm trees, and
warm ocean breezes seem a million miles away, drown yourself in a drink guaranteed to be more blue than you.

Good Drink: *Blue Hawaiian*

1 ounce light rum
1 ounce blue curaçao
2 ounces pineapple juice
1 ounce cream of coconut
Pineapple slice and maraschino cherry for garnish

Combine the rum, curaçao, pineapple juice, and cream of coconut with one cup of crushed ice in a blender at high speed. Pour into highball glass. Garnish with pineapple slice and cherry. Drink while listening to Elvis.

Bad Day: *Pressure from meddlesome parents*

No one can get under your skin like your parents. It doesn't matter if you're fourteen or forty, they still like to tell you how to live your life. And for some reason, the holidays kick their interrogations into high gear. They can't seem to resist asking pointed questions about every possible aspect of your life. Are you seeing anyone special? Have you landed that promotion? Can you really afford that car? Have you *finally* finished your dissertation? Why aren't you wearing that lovely hat that your cousin knitted for you? Luckily, this simple yet fiery cocktail will help you endure one more family meal on the hot seat.

Good Drink: *Third Degree*

1½ ounces gin
1 teaspoon Sambuca or anisette
¾ ounce dry vermouth

Shake gin, Sambuca, and vermouth with ice, then strain into a cocktail glass. Drink while practicing your best "yes, ma'am" and "no, sir" without sighing.

From Bad to Worse: Are you still being compared (unfavorably) to your siblings? Make it a double—and make one more for your parental unit!

Bad Day: *Caught the flu*

It's one thing to have a pesky winter cold. It's another to become truly ill. You've tried it all: ice packs, heating pads, chicken soup, dry toast, daytime TV. None of it makes you feel better. You're so sick, you almost wish you were well enough to go to work! When nothing seems to cure what ails you, try a tea strong enough to render those germs unconscious. If possible, have a friend, loved one, or even your mom make it for you and deliver it to the bathtub!

Good Drink: *Blueberry Tea*

1 ounce Grand Marnier or Cointreau
1 ounce amaretto
Orange pekoe tea
Orange wheel for garnish

Pour the Grand Marnier and amaretto into a preheated brandy snifter. Fill the snifter two-thirds of the way to the top with orange pekoe tea. Stir and garnish with orange wheel.

From Bad to Worse: Did you actually get a flu shot and *still* get the flu? Take two doses and off to bed!

Bad Day: *Can't assemble gift*

It is nearly midnight on Christmas Eve. And naturally, the must-have bike/playhouse/train set is only now coming out of its packaging. Why didn't anyone tell you assembly was required? And why didn't the box indicate that the process would require seventeen tools you don't even own? When the pressure is on, it's best to refresh yourself with a drink that's impossible to screw up.

Good Drink: *Screwdriver*

1½ ounces vodka
5 ounces orange juice

Pour vodka and orange juice into an ice-filled highball glass and stir.

From Bad to Worse: Are the instructions in another language? Make it a Cordless Screwdriver: chill the vodka in the freezer and drink it as a shot, then follow up with a chomp of a sugar-coated orange wedge.

Bad Day: *Got back together with ex out of holiday desperation*

Here you go again! Somehow, you have found yourself back together with the one person who made you swear, "Never again!" Perhaps you just wanted a date for the office party this year. Perchance you got weepy while watching *It's a Wonderful Life* for the umpteenth time. Or maybe a devastating combination of holiday weddings, diamond ads, family pressure, and too much eggnog precipitated the fatal phone call. Whatever the circumstances, there's no denying the fact that the holidays make us sentimental . . . and sometimes, just plain blind. Turn off that inner voice with a drink that's all about the do-over.

Good Drink: *Boomerang*

1 ounce dry vermouth
1½ ounces gin
Dash of bitters
Dash of maraschino juice (from jar of cherries)
Lemon peel for garnish

Stir vermouth, gin, bitters, and maraschino juice with ice, then strain into a chilled cocktail glass. Add a twist of lemon peel in the shape of a boomerang.

Bad Day: *Credit card declined*

Everyone goes broke during the holidays, right? You knew you were maybe a little over your budget, but you had no idea how far off you really were. That is, until your card was soundly declined at a department store—right in front of a long line of annoyed customers with actual funds. You not only had to endure the embarrassment, you had to leave all those gifts behind! Now what? Time to break out the glue gun and the pipe cleaners; looks like those left on your list are getting homemade presents this year. Remember, it's the thought that counts!

Good Drink: *Park Avenue*

1 ½ ounces gin
¼ ounce sweet vermouth
¼ ounce dry vermouth
¼ ounce pineapple juice

Stir gin, sweet vermouth, dry vermouth, and pineapple juice with ice, then strain into cocktail glass. Drink while hunting for change under your couch cushions.

Bad Day: *Holiday hangover*

Hangovers that come from holiday drinks seem especially brutal. Packed with alcohol, sugar, and even heavy cream, beverages that seem decadent and delicious at the time can really do a number on you the following morning. And speaking of numbers, just how many trips to the punch bowl did you make, anyway? If you have a vague recollection of blowing your Christmas money on drinks for the whole bar or whispering something R-rated into Santa's ear, you probably had one too many. Time for just one more!

Good Drink: *Eye Opener*

2 ounces dark rum
½ teaspoon orange curaçao
½ teaspoon apricot brandy
1 teaspoon grenadine
1 egg yolk

Shake rum, curaçao, brandy, grenadine, and egg yolk (quietly) with ice, then strain into a cocktail glass. Drink with the hand not holding the ice pack to your head.

Bad Day: *Last-minute quest for sold-out gift*

You can't believe you've become one of those people who go to the mall in the middle of the night. Ever the optimist, you promised your favorite niece or nephew a particular toy months ago. Of course you could get it! Piece of cake! Now, it's two days before Christmas and the coveted item is sold-out . . . everywhere. So, like an idiot, you've joined the hordes of frazzled shoppers running from one megastore to the next, scouring the shelves in vain. Good thing everything is open late. You're going to need some sustenance to keep up this pace.

Good Drink: *Midnight Express*

1½ ounces dark rum
½ ounce Cointreau
¾ ounce lime juice
1 splash sour mix

Shake rum, Cointreau, lime juice, and sour mix with ice, then pour over ice into an old-fashioned glass. Drink while searching online stores.

From Bad to Worse: **Did you find it online but have to pay ridiculous rush postage? Double the rum!**

Bad Day: *No Christmas bonus*

Sure, you know a bonus isn't "guaranteed." But when you get a nice check every year, you start to count on it. Then you start to factor it into your holiday budget. Maybe you've even already spent it—two months ago! Meanwhile, the only envelope your boss offered you this year contained a photo Christmas card of his family skiing in Aspen. It's so unfair! At least you can indulge in this little luxury. It may be the only one you have for a while!

Good Drink: *Luxury*

3 ounces brandy
2 dashes orange bitters
3 ounces chilled champagne

Pour brandy, bitters, and champagne into a champagne flute and stir gently. Drink while taking a personal day.

Bad Day: *Grand gesture backfires*

Way to go—you really put yourself out there. Was it a candlelit proposal? An over-the-top gift? A truckload of long-stemmed roses? A faithful reenactment of your first date? A lovingly prepared six-course meal? If your sweetie seemed under-whelmed (or scared, or annoyed) with your deluxe display, you're likely feeling unappreciated, disappointed, and most of all, thirsty. Soothe the sting of defeat with a classic remedy.

Good Drink: *Stinger*

½ ounce white crème de menthe
1½ ounces brandy

Shake crème de menthe and brandy with ice, then strain into a chilled cocktail glass. Drink while planning your next move.

From Bad to Worse: Was your gesture not only romantic but expensive? Double the brandy and rent *Say Anything*.

Bad Day: *Christmas decorations cause power outage*

Who isn't inspired by watching yet another rerun of *National Lampoon's Christmas Vacation*? If a bumbling Chevy Chase can illuminate his entire house, surely you can figure it out. So you spent a fortune on twinkling lights, electric candy canes, and an enormous animated Santa to pop in and out of your chimney all night long. You're in the holiday spirit! Or at least you were until all the power went out. Ah well, drink a couple of these . . . and at least *you* will be lit up, Sparky!

Good Drink: *Electric Iced Tea*

½ ounce bourbon
½ ounce vodka
½ ounce gin
½ ounce triple sec
3 to 4 ounces cola
2 lemon wedges

Pour bourbon, vodka, gin, triple sec, and cola over ice into a highball glass. Squeeze in lemon wedges and stir. Make a second round quickly, before all the ice in your freezer begins to melt.

From Bad to Worse: Is your frozen turkey (and all the fixings) now room temperature? Double the bourbon and remember, there's always takeout.

Bad Day: *Inappropriate hookup*

The holidays made you do it! Whether it was a former employee, your sibling's ex, a formerly platonic roommate, or just a random person you met on the bus, you went where you really, really should not have gone. Now you're dodging phone calls, denying it to your friends, and trying to erase the images from your mind. Hey, it's the holidays—a few acts of crazy are allowed. So, what the hell . . . just have a stiff drink and embrace it!

Good Drink: *What the Hell*

1 ounce gin
1 ounce dry vermouth
1 ounce apricot-flavored brandy
Dash of lemon juice

Pour gin, vermouth, brandy, and lemon juice into an ice-filled old-fashioned glass and stir.

From Bad to Worse: Was your hookup partner still involved with someone else? Double the gin!

Bad Day: *Terrible weather*

Why can't the holidays be scheduled in the summer? Aren't they stressful enough without adding freezing temperatures, icy roads, and snow? No matter how many layers of Christmas sweaters you put on, you can't seem to shake the bone-chilling cold. And no matter how much you try to embrace the beauty of winter, all you can think of is running away to Hawaii. Time to fire up the furnace, put on your sunglasses, and warm up with a drink that's (sing it with me!) like a heat wave, burning in your heart.

Good Drink: *Heat Wave*

1½ ounces coconut rum
½ ounce peach schnapps
3 ounces pineapple juice
3 ounces orange juice
½ ounce grenadine

Pour rum, schnapps, pineapple juice, and orange juice over ice into a traditional hurricane or wine glass. Top with grenadine. Drink under a sunlamp.

Bad Day: *Must bare pasty body on vacation*

You're super happy to be on vacation this holiday season. Sure, you had to deal with expensive tickets, horrible airport lines, delayed flights, and an overpriced hotel room, but it was all worth it. Alas, there's one more drawback. In return for balmy weather and blue skies, you have to do something . . . well, horrifying. You have to wear a swimsuit! Chances are, your body has not seen the light of day in many months, so brace yourself: you are in for a shock. If the first glance in the mirror evokes thoughts of the Michelin Man, Pillsbury Dough Boy, or another pale and pudgy animated creature, you're going to need some liquid courage to take the long walk from your beach towel to the water. Dip into this.

Good Drink: *Skinny Dipper*

2 ounces Midori melon liqueur
6 ounces cranberry juice

Pour Midori and cranberry juice over ice into a highball glass.
Drink while applying self-tanner and sucking in.

Bad Day: *Busted for flirting at holiday party*

It's totally unfair. Your date chatted up all sorts of eligibles without any repercussions. You did just a wee bit of harmless flirting, and you got called on it! Sure, the person you were talking to was particularly attractive. And maybe there was some extraneous giggling, touching, and hair tossing—on both sides. But you were only being friendly! Face it, there's simply no reasoning with a jealous mate at holiday time. Just take solace in the fact that you're right, and drink to the unfairness of love's little rules.

Good Drink: *Double Standard Sour*

¾ ounce whiskey
¾ ounce gin
¾ ounce fresh lemon juice
½ ounce simple syrup (see page 3)
Dash of grenadine
Lemon slice and maraschino cherry for garnish

Shake the whiskey, gin, lemon juice, simple syrup, and grenadine vigorously with ice, then strain into a chilled sour glass, or serve over ice in an old-fashioned glass. Garnish with lemon slice and cherry.

Bad Day: *Slipped on ice*

You probably had your arms full of shopping bags. Chances are, you were on your way to or from the mall/grocery store/ airport for the umpteenth time this season. But this time, your feet just flew out from under you like a couple of novice reindeer. If you're lucky, you'll just need some Advil and an ice pack. But if your little sidewalk spill means a trip to the emergency room, a splint, or even a cast, you deserve a drink that's a truly potent painkiller.

Good Drink: *Singapore Sling*

Juice of ½ lemon
1 teaspoon powdered sugar
2 ounces gin
Club soda
½ ounce cherry-flavored brandy

Shake lemon, sugar, and gin with ice and strain into a high-ball glass. Add ice cubes and fill with soda. Float the brandy on top. Serve with a straw and sip while soaking in an Epsom salts bath.

Bad Day: *Annoying relatives in town*

The more the merrier? Not exactly. But there's nothing like a houseful of surly relatives to make the holidays . . . *interesting*. Everyone has an opinion, no one helps with the dishes, and there are even people sleeping in your bed. If your duties as host involve chauffeuring, catering, and playing tour guide to out-of-towners, and you still haven't cracked under the pressure, you deserve a reward. Since a peaceful night's sleep may not be on the table until after your guests leave, embrace the coming of the night with this nocturnal nectar.

Good Drink: *Nightmare*

1½ ounces gin
½ ounce Madeira
½ ounce cherry-flavored brandy
1 teaspoon orange juice

Shake gin, Madeira, brandy, and orange juice with ice, then strain into a cocktail glass. Drink under the cover of darkness.

From Bad to Worse: Do you live in a studio apartment? Forget the extras and just sip straight gin!

Bad Day: *Caught sweetie smooching someone else under the mistletoe*

You thought things were going well. So well, in fact, that you decided it was time to debut your new love interest at *the* holiday party of the season. Surprise! You turn your back for a moment . . . and your current squeeze is squeezing someone else. Maybe "holiday cheer" was trotted out as an excuse, but you can't blame mistletoe for a kiss like that. Mend your broken heart with this sweet elixir.

Good Drink: *Heartbreaker's Special*

2 ounces vodka

2 ounces passion fruit liqueur

1 ounce pineapple juice

1 ounce orange juice

1 orange

Pour vodka, passion fruit liqueur, pineapple juice, and orange juice into blender. Add one scoop of crushed ice and flesh from orange. Blend until smooth and pour into a highball glass.

From Bad to Worse: **Was it not only a surprising person, but a surprising gender? Double the vodka!**

Bad Day: *Gained weight*

Gingerbread cookies. Homemade fudge. Candy canes. Fruit-cake. Stuffing. Gravy. Eggnog! It's no wonder everyone packs on the pounds during the holidays. But the first time you step on the scale, it can still hurt. (Think of how the scale feels, ha ha ha!) Rest assured, you are not alone. Virtually everyone in America gains seven pounds between Thanksgiving and New Year's. And the solstice season is no time to diet. So heat up those leftovers, unwrap another chocolate Santa, and indulge in a decadent drink that will be a distant memory by Memorial Day.

Good Drink: *Hot Buttered Rum*

1 teaspoon brown sugar
Boiling water
1 tablespoon butter
2 ounces dark rum
Dash of nutmeg

Put sugar into a mug and fill two-thirds full with boiling water. Add butter and rum. Stir and sprinkle with nutmeg.

From Bad to Worse: Can't even fit into your "fat pants"? Might as well double the butter—what difference can it make now?

Bad Day: *Forced home for holidays*

Are you sleeping in your tiny childhood bed? Enduring passive-aggressive comments from your parents? Being tormented by your siblings? Oh, there's no place like home. Aren't you glad you didn't go to Cabo with your friends? It's bad enough that you're stuck in your cold, dreary hometown for the holidays. But all your family members under the same roof again, as adults? It's enough to make anyone blow a gasket. Time to mix yourself a drink—even if you have to sneak into the kitchen after everyone's asleep in order to avoid the disapproving looks.

Good Drink: *Short Fuse*

2 ounces gold tequila
½ ounce apricot brandy
1½ ounces fresh lime juice
3 ounces fresh grapefruit juice
¼ ounce maraschino cherry juice (from a jar of cherries)
Lime wedge

Shake the tequila, brandy, lime juice, grapefruit juice, and cherry juice with ice, then strain into an ice-filled highball glass. Squeeze the lime wedge over the drink and drop it in. Drink while repeating to yourself, "I *am* an adult."

From Bad to Worse: Is your significant other staying down the hall, even though you're over 21? Add a tequila floater!

Bad Day: *Office party debacle*

Ho ho ho! Blame it on the mistletoe, the strong drinks, or the lack of real food, but someone got a bit nutty at the office holiday party. Did you dirty dance with an intern? Photocopy a body part? Spill something on the CEO? Your only hope is that everyone else was similarly over served and underfed—maybe the night is a blur to them, too. Better cross your fingers that you're not on everyone's camera phones this morning!

Good Drink: *Morning After*

2 ounces Pernod
1 teaspoon Sambuca
1 egg white
1 to 2 ounces chilled club soda

Shake the Pernod, Sambuca, and egg white vigorously with ice, then strain into an ice-filled old-fashioned glass. Add the club soda and stir gently.

From Bad to Worse: Did you wake up in your cubicle? Sip a second round while updating your resume!

Bad Day: *Relationship on the rocks*

The holidays put tremendous strain on any relationship.
Stress levels are up, commitments crowd the calendar, and
there's no doubt that someone bought the wrong gift or said
the wrong thing at an important social gathering. It's a lot of
pressure! If you find that your significant other is giving you
the cold shoulder, it's time to take a break. Unplug the phone
and keep yourself warm with a decadent cold drink guaranteed to help you chill.

Good Drink: *The Big Chill*

4 ounces chilled coffee
1 ounce coffee liqueur
1 ounce cream
1 ounce dark rum
½ teaspoon sugar
1 scoop vanilla ice cream

Shake coffee, coffee liqueur, cream, rum, and sugar with ice, then strain into a highball glass and top with ice cream. Serve with a straw and a long spoon.

> **From Bad to Worse: Did you give a really expensive gift, and then break up? Add a rum floater before topping with ice cream.**

Bad Day: *Annoyed by carolers*

As if it's not bad enough being inundated by annoying holiday music at every party and in every store and elevator— now it has to come to your friggin' door? You've endured all the decorations. Your neighbor's blinking lights. The incessant ringing of bells. The terrible holiday specials on TV. The Santa movies at the Cineplex. But really, this is the last straw. In today's litigious world, it's probably not wise to throw an actual snowball at the perpetrators singing yet another round of "Here Comes Santa Claus" on your doorstep. But thankfully, you can still throw one in your own direction.

Good Drink: *Snowball*

2 ounces brandy

1 ounce simple syrup (see page 3)

1 egg

3 to 4 ounces ginger ale

Shake the brandy, simple syrup, and egg vigorously with ice, then strain into an ice-filled cocktail glass. Top with ginger ale to taste. Drink while humming any song that is not holiday related.

Bad Day: *Spent hours in long lines*

The post office. The toy store. The department store. The returns counter. You have literally spent most of your day in line, only to end it sitting in a line of cars trying to get home. Argh! This is no time to queue up at a bar or party, trying desperately to get served. Cancel any plans that might involve waiting for anything from anybody, go home, and immediately pour yourself a drink that is the antidote to your paralyzing day.

Good Drink: *Paralyzer*

1 ounce Kahlúa
½ ounce vodka
1 ounce cola
2 to 3 ounces milk

Pour Kahlúa, vodka, and cola into an ice-filled old-fashioned glass. Add milk to taste and stir gently.

Bad Day: *Holiday indigestion*

You honestly can't remember the last time you ate a crisp vegetable or piece of fresh fruit. For the last few weeks, anything remotely resembling produce has been smothered under heavy cream, marshmallows, brown sugar, gravy, cream of mushroom soup, or all of the above. Your belly is *not* happy. Forget milk of magnesia . . . instead, turn to a cocktail that does double duty.

Good Drink: *Smooth Move*

1 ounce rum
2 ounces pineapple juice
2 ounces prune juice
2 ounces sour mix
Pineapple spear and maraschino cherry for garnish

Combine rum, pineapple juice, prune juice, and sour mix in blender with ice and blend until smooth. Pour into a sugar-rimmed cocktail glass. Garnish with pineapple spear and cherry.

Bad Day: *Failed to impress future in-laws*

You were assured that they would *love* you. That they were easygoing, open-minded, *normal*. And so, you went boldly to meet your significant other's family at some huge holiday gathering. But somehow, things went awry. Did you make an inappropriate joke? Put your elbow in the gravy? Wear the totally wrong thing? Accidentally insult the matriarch? Whatever your faux pas, if you want to smooth things over, it's going to take some serious charm (also known as sucking up). Suck this down first. At least your drink will be debonair.

Good Drink: *Debonair*

2 ounces single-malt scotch
1 ounce ginger liqueur
Lemon twist

Shake the scotch and liqueur vigorously with ice and strain
into a cocktail glass. Twist the lemon over the drink and drop
it in.

Bad Day: *Post-party mess*

Oh, is there any hell quite as dark as the morning after a party? Your head hurts. Your teeth are numb. And your place is a pigsty! Empty glasses, full ashtrays, crushed hors d'oeuvres, dirty dishes, and a particularly heinous smell that can only be attributed to the day-old pigs in a blanket near the space heater. If you want to survive the day, you have no alternative but to roll your sleeves up and get dirty. Dirty martini, that is.

Good Drink: *Dirty Martini*

2 ounces gin
½ ounce extra-dry vermouth
½ ounce brine from cocktail olives
Green cocktail olive for garnish

Stir the gin, vermouth, and brine with ice, then strain into a chilled cocktail glass. Garnish with olive and get to work.

> **From Bad to Worse: Was the party totally lame to boot? Make it a double and call a cleaning service.**

Bad Day: *Totally stressed out*

The noise. The crowds. The mall. The relatives. The gift you can't find. The packages you haven't mailed. The family headaches. The end-of-year deadlines. It's just too much! When the holidays are on your last nerve, it's time to chill out with a completely nonseasonal drink. No eggnog, no champagne, no brandy . . . just a relaxing cocktail to lower your anxiety level. At least for today.

Good Drink: *Rum Relaxer*

1½ ounces light rum
1 ounce pineapple juice
½ ounce grenadine
3 to 5 ounces lemon-lime soda
Orange slice and cherry for garnish

Shake rum, pineapple juice, and grenadine with ice and strain into an ice-filled highball glass. Add lemon-lime soda to taste and garnish with orange slice and cherry. Drink while taking deep, cleansing breaths.

Bad Day: *Must pretend to like awful present*

You're no stranger to faking enthusiasm. In fact, you think you're pretty darn good at it. But unwrapping a large, much-anticipated gift and then managing to act thrilled about a heinous reindeer sweater, outdated electronics item, or insanely awful piece of art? That's a skill. And like many skills, it is better honed while slightly buzzed. So take a cue from the Irish, masters in the art of BS, who believe that a visit to the Blarney Stone blesses you with the gift of gab. Since you probably can't get to the real thing, try the liquid version. You're going to need it.

Good Drink: *Blarney Stone*

2 ounces Irish whiskey
¼ ounce Cointreau
¼ ounce Pernod or anisette
Dash of maraschino liqueur
Dash of angostura bitters
Lemon twist

Stir the whiskey, Cointreau, Pernod, and maraschino liqueur with ice, then strain into a chilled cocktail glass. Run the lemon peel around the rim, twist it over the drink, and drop it in. Sip while saying, "I love it!" with feeling.

Bad Day: *Holiday travel woes*

It never fails. Trips you take the rest of the year may be totally smooth and uneventful, but holiday travel will make you crazy. Your luggage will be lost. Your flight will be canceled. Your rental car will be MIA. Your security line will be the slowest. No matter what route you decide to take, it will be the wrong one. And all along the way, you'll run into snow, fog, sleet, crowds, and travelers even grumpier than you. It's enough to send you into a . . . you guessed it. When you finally make it to your destination, you've earned one of these.

Good Drink: *Tailspin*

¾ ounce gin
¾ ounce sweet vermouth
¾ ounce Chartreuse
Dash of orange bitters
Lemon peel

Stir gin, vermouth, Chartreuse, and bitters with ice, then strain into a cocktail glass. Twist the lemon over the drink and drop it in. Sip while repeating, "There's no place like home, there's no place like home."

Bad Day: *Screwed up holiday meal*

Somehow, it's four o'clock in the afternoon and the turkey is still frozen. You burned the pie. Forgot the rolls. Didn't realize that potatoes actually have to be cooked before you mash them. Or maybe you were so focused on drinks and appetizers that you forgot about the main course altogether. Now you have a houseful of hungry people and absolutely nothing edible to serve them. Give them plenty of rounds of this drink (while assuring them dinner is coming), and they may forgive you . . . or even forget that you didn't feed them.

Good Drink: *Thanksgiving Special*

¾ ounce apricot-flavored brandy

¾ ounce gin

¾ ounce dry vermouth

¼ teaspoon lemon juice

Maraschino cherry for garnish

Shake brandy, gin, vermouth, and lemon juice with ice, then strain into a cocktail glass. Serve with a cherry—and plenty of cheese and crackers.

Bad Day: *Coal in stocking*

Sometimes, no matter how much you tell yourself to grow up,
Christmas causes flashbacks of being eight years old and find-
ing socks instead of a new bike under the tree. It's a holiday
that sets you up for disappointment, no matter how moderate
your hopes. And you can't help but feel bratty about it. So,
what to do when you're this mad at Santa? Eat his cookies
and spike your eggnog! At least now that you're over 21, you
can enjoy this kind of sweet revenge.

Good Drink: *Brandy Eggnog*

1½ ounces brandy
½ ounce tawny port
3½ ounces whole milk
¾ ounce cream
¼ ounce simple syrup (see page 3)
1 egg yolk
Dash of nutmeg

Shake brandy, port, milk, cream, simple syrup, and egg yolk vigorously with ice, then strain into ice-filled highball glass. Top with nutmeg, and drink while ordering yourself the perfect stocking stuffer online.

(Need a shortcut? Don't like the idea of raw egg? Just add the brandy to store-bought 'nog and top with nutmeg.)

Bad Day: *No date for New Year's*

New Year's Eve can be the worst. So much pressure! You have to think about where to go, how to get there, what to wear, and . . . oh yeah, you have no date. You may be wondering, what good is a party invitation with no one to kiss at midnight? *Au contraire!* Remember, sometimes no date is better than the wrong date. And who knows, maybe you'll end up with someone else's escort! So put on your party clothes, go boldly stag, and pucker up with the only kiss guaranteed not to disappoint.

Good Drink: *Kiss on the Lips*

2 ounces bourbon
6 ounces apricot nectar

Pour bourbon and nectar over ice into a highball glass and stir. Serve with a straw. Drink while applying lip balm. Kiss the old year goodbye!

REMEDIES FOR THE REST OF THE YEAR

If you survived the holiday season from Thanksgiving to New Year's, congratulations. That's not an easy feat! Hopefully, some strategic cocktail consumption helped pull you through. Still, you just might need a little help during the rest of the year, too. Here are a few suggestions to guide you through those holidays that may be less stressful but are certainly no less deserving of a drink.

Bad Day: *Alone on Valentine's Day*

Whether you're weathering a recent breakup or have been solo for ages, this is one holiday that strikes fear in the hearts of all singles. No matter how much you tell yourself not to let it get to you, you are assaulted by "love" at every turn. You must endure the sight of endless boxes of candy, cupid-covered window displays, romantic movie ads, and hearts, hearts, hearts. If you're dealing with a broken one, you're understandably bitter. No need to sugarcoat things—instead, treat yourself to a bracing cocktail that is anything but saccharin.

Good Drink: *Bitters & Soda*

4 to 6 ounces chilled club soda
2 to 3 dashes angostura or other bitters

Pour the club soda into an ice-filled highball glass. Add a few dashes of bitters and stir briefly.

Bad Day: *Went broke at Presidents' Day sales*

What better way to celebrate our nation's forefathers than with discounted flat-screen TVs and designer boots? Somehow, it's become traditional to beat the February blues by parting with all of your green. If you're surprised to realize that sale prices enticed you into spending all your Christmas dough in one long weekend, you're likely feeling some buyer's remorse. Tell yourself that you're just selflessly helping to stimulate the economy. Like Lincoln and Washington, you're doing it for your country!

Good Drink: *Greenback*

1½ ounces gin
¼ ounce crème de menthe
½ ounce fresh lime juice
2 to 3 ounces chilled club soda

Shake the gin, crème de menthe, and lime juice with ice, then strain into an ice-filled highball glass. Top with club soda.

Bad Day: *Overindulged on St. Patrick's Day*

You were just innocently celebrating a beloved cultural holiday. Who can remember when the black and tans became Irish whiskeys, neat? Or when you started kissing everyone in the bar who claimed to be Irish? If you woke up not only wearing green, but feeling green, then it's high time to put on a pot of coffee and have a little hair of the Irish setter that bit you.

Good Drink: *Irish Coffee*

1½ ounces Irish whiskey
1 teaspoon brown sugar
5 to 6 ounces strong, hot coffee
Heavy cream or whipped cream

Pour the whiskey into a warmed mug or Irish coffee glass, then add the brown sugar and stir until dissolved. Pour in the hot coffee. Slowly add the cream to float on top, or top with a dollop of whipped cream.

Bad Day: *Sugar cravings caused by Easter Bunny*

Cadbury Creme Eggs. Chocolate bunnies. Marshmallow chicks. Even if you don't have kids, you can't turn your back on Easter treats. In fact, you've consumed so much sugar that your hands are now too shaky to dye eggs. If you don't know how you're going to get through each post-Easter day without biting the ears off a chocolate rabbit, switch up your vices and trade sugar for alcohol. Hop over to this vivid cocktail; it will put a whole new spring in your step.

Good Drink: *Spring Feeling*

1 ounce gin
½ ounce green Chartreuse
1 tablespoon fresh lemon juice

Shake gin, Chartreuse, and lemon juice with ice, then strain into a chilled cocktail glass.

Bad Day: *Forgot to call mom on Mother's Day*

You were enjoying a leisurely spring Sunday when, at eleven o'clock at night, it hit you: it's Mother's Day! You didn't send flowers, you didn't write, you didn't even *call*. How could the universe let this happen? Rest assured, you will be punished— and no one punishes you like mom. You'll be sending long-stemmed roses for a decade! In the meantime, start crafting a really airtight excuse—like perhaps you were on a remote tropical island with no phone service? This drink will help inspire you.

Good Drink: *Bahama Mama*

1 ounce dark rum
½ ounce coconut rum
½ ounce coffee liqueur
4 ounces pineapple juice
1½ ounces fresh lemon juice
1 tablespoon 151-proof rum
Pineapple wedge and maraschino cherry for garnish

Shake dark rum, coconut rum, coffee liqueur, pineapple juice, and lemon juice vigorously with ice, then strain into chilled cocktail glass. Float the 151 on top. Garnish with pineapple wedge and cherry. Sip while planning a suitably grand gesture for tomorrow.

Bad Day: *Beach mishap on Memorial Day*

You were so eager to get out to the beach for the holiday weekend. It seemed like a great idea. So what went wrong? Did you have a swimsuit malfunction? Get a truly weird sunburn? Capsize a friend's boat? Realize that everyone else is younger and fitter than you? Let's face it: the beach is over-rated. Time to stay indoors and cool off with a cocktail that requires no SPF protection.

Good Drink: *Splash & Crash*

2 ounces amaretto
6 ounces cranberry juice
2 ounces orange juice
½ ounce 151-proof rum
Lime wheel for garnish

Pour amaretto, cranberry juice, and orange juice over ice into
a highball glass. Top with 151 and garnish with lime wheel.
Drink *before* trying to extricate sand from all the places it really
shouldn't be.

Bad Day: *Accidentally bested dad on Father's Day*

Checkmate the old man in seven moves? Sink that 40-foot putt to beat him on the links? Get to HORSE before he even sank one ball? Finish the crossword first? Only one question remains now: *what were you thinking?* You know dad loves to win, and today of all days, you should have let him. As far as presents go, a victory is better than another necktie. Snap him out of his poor-sport funk by making him an offer he can't refuse: a drink to celebrate the man who will always be head of the family.

Good Drink: *Godfather*

2 ounces scotch or bourbon

1 ounce amaretto

Shake scotch and amaretto with ice, then strain into an ice-filled old-fashioned glass. Drink while graciously accepting dad's constructive criticism on your job, attire, and life goals.

Bad Day: *Faulty fireworks on Independence Day*

Booze and fireworks aren't usually the smartest combination—a fact everyone seems to forget on the Fourth of July. Did you burn your fingers on sparklers? Launch a sidewinder into your neighbor's yard? Set the roof on fire? Well, chalk it up to the patriotic spirit of the holiday; rocket's red glare and all that. Just try to at least keep the barbecue—and the bar—from going up in flames.

Good Drink: *Stars & Stripes*

²/₃ ounce grenadine syrup

²/₃ ounce heavy cream

²/₃ ounce blue curaçao

Layer syrup, cream, and curaçao into a cordial or wine glass.
Drink while enjoying a nicely charred hot dog.

Bad Day: *Labor Day traffic jams*

When summer vacation season comes to a close, people get a little crazy. What else could account for everyone hitting the freeways at once? It's against all semblance of reason. And yet, you were so eager to get to the beach/mountains/lake/airport that you joined the fray. Along the way, you witnessed some really, truly terrible driving (from the person right in front of you, of course). When you do make it to your destination, have the only California driver you'll ever appreciate.

Good Drink: *California Driver*

1 ounce vodka

3 ounces grapefruit juice

3 ounces orange juice

Pour the vodka, grapefruit juice, and orange juice over ice into a highball glass and stir gently.

Bad Day: *Got tricked on Halloween*

Sure, Halloween pranks are hilarious when you're a kid. But if you're of cocktail-drinking age, rotten eggs in your mailbox, toilet paper in your trees, or smashed pumpkins on your porch can be a real drag. And having to deal with the mess while nursing a killer candy hangover? Now that's scary. Nothing left to do but put on a brave face, open another "fun size" Snickers bar, and mix a drink that's just right for this dark holiday.

Good Drink: *Black Magic*

1 ½ ounces vodka
¾ ounce Kahlúa
Dash of fresh lemon juice
Lemon twist

Shake the vodka, Kahlúa, and lemon juice vigorously with ice, then strain into an ice-filled old-fashioned glass. Twist the lemon peel over the drink and drop it in. Drink while polishing off anything left in the candy bowl and turning off the porch light.

Bad Day: *Things didn't go your way on Election Day*

No matter who prevails on Election Day, the aftermath can hit hard. You might be angry and disappointed, or relieved but nervous. Either way, you are undoubtedly sick of the ads, speeches, debates, and watercooler conjecture. Enough already! Can't everyone just go back to talking about *Top Chef* and where they're going for vacation? Bid adieu to the grueling election season with this powerful pick-me-up of a cocktail.

Good Drink: *American Dream*

¼ ounce coffee liqueur

¼ ounce amaretto

¼ ounce hazelnut liqueur

¼ ounce dark crème de cacao

Chill coffee liqueur, amaretto, hazelnut liqueur, and crème de cacao with ice, then strain into a shot glass. Toast to the next four years!

Index

About the Author

Kerry Colburn is a freelance writer who lives and drinks in Seattle, where her family, friends, and well-stocked bar guard against foul moods. She's the author of *Good Drinks for Bad Days*, as well as *The U.S. of Eh?: How Canada Secretly Controls the United States*, which she co-authored with her husband, Rob Sorensen.